EXPLICATIONS/INTERPRETATIONS

D0627971

The publication of this volume is supported in part by a grant from the Kentucky Arts Council with funds from the National Endowment for the Arts.

Books by Jay Wright (*in order written*)

Death as History (Poets Press, 1967)

The Homecoming Singer (Corinth, 1971)

Soothsayers and Omens (Seven Woods Press, 1976)

Explications/Interpretations (Callaloo Poetry Series, 1984)

Dimensions of History (Kayak, 1976)

The Double Invention of Komo (University of Texas Press, 1980)

EXPLICATIONS/INTERPRETATIONS

Jay Wright

Volume Three
in the Callaloo Poetry Series
Published at the University of Kentucky
Lexington, 1984

Some of the poems in this volume first appeared in the
following publications:

"The Sunset's Widow," *American Poetry Review*
"The Body," *Yardbird Reader*
"Twenty-Two Tremblings," 1-12, *Hambone*
"Love's Dozen," *Massachusetts Review* and *Chant of
Saints*
"MacIntyre, the Captain and the Saints," *TriQuarterly*
"The Continuing City: Spirit and Body" (read at Library of
Congress)

Detail from "Ojo de Dios," front cover art, by Tomás
Coffeen-Suhl; photographed by William R. Deal.

ISBN: 0-912759-01-1

CALLALOO POETRY SERIES
University of Kentucky
Lexington, Kentucky 40506-0027

For
Harold Bloom
and
Robert Hayden

"Juana" by Tomás Coffeen-Suhl

CONTENTS

TENSIONS AND RESOLUTIONS

At dawn, the pips
are piped up by the birds
to watch the night woman
tune and take her lover's arms.
It is such a small
and almost silent beginning
that there seem to be no measure,
no assertions of stars, fire bursts,
prophetic serpents, clamor of shells
ripped from the river, no whisper
of wind to husk in the wet field.
We say each dawn is a bond
of your own beginning,
the ground established for our
movement from dawn to dawn.
Clearly, we must remember,
just at that moment—
the confusion of light
of first star and first sun.
Every appearance
rises in its clarity of bones,
flesh, leaf, trunk and skin,
turns toward its proper placement of light,
the space it places clearly about its body.
Each moment lives two lives in its act.
Each act caresses
the moment it remembers,
and the moment it desires.
Outside our love,
the night woman,
image of our flesh-gifted saints,
lingers, silent and serene,
to hear the women
beat their earthy bowls,
and worry us with time.
Spirit-skilled,
we still cannot escape
these solid claims,
the inhabitable body sprung
from its debt of stillness.

10

Here, we live, at rest,
a throng of acts,
propped up by the constant caress
of a movement,
search in the light of first star
and first sun,
for a sound and an act
to acknowledge.

POLARITY'S TRIO

ZONES

In the city of eternal spring
I awake in a mist and lay
my arepa on the buttered air.
Then, in the zone of healing water,
I take my jangada and ride,
Maracucho, on the pulse of your blood,
the black *ir-venir* of the bay's clock.
Jangada, sloop, coracle, skiff, a shell,
we all have nets, bright silver shawls,
to enfold the water at dawn.
We rehearse an old Mexican prayer;
the fish kick and sprinkle the shore.
This is the bitter beginning
of a flood day, or a drought,
the ticking of the jaguar's teeth.
Plain marble murmurs—
dress my master in liliquiqui,
twist the bulls' tails, dance,
four in four,
to the harp and the snake's bones.
I am entranced by Maracaibo,
steel leg in the air—
plunge, the exaltation.
All day, from dawn, I scrape
the soft scales of little fish,
or pluck the veins and little bones
of my brown mother's body,
or cuddle my own weaver's call
                              in the market.
I reward my hunger with a toothpick of hide.
I will sleep,
and think of the liquid black hardness
that bleeds the marrow of my bones.
Some god will flood the ocean's night
with an echo of my morning.
We work,
with the body's changing firmness,
to repair the constancy of things.

CORRIDA

Trumpets at four o'clock
seal the rain in the Plaza.
    All capes are darker.
Spangles choke their novilleros,
who wait in the blood the water soaks
from the Plaza's shallow blood urn.
The rain eases nothing.
Left-handed bulls shoot for the center,
hook the guards, tumble blind horses.

In the infinity of one faena,
one cherub learns the rigor of space.
     Pic and call.
     The night horn.
The daemon flourishes his flags.
Hovering at the wing,
he would ride the loose gestures
      into the cherub's body,
ride down into the nerve song we ask of it.
All in a circle of fire,
angels fan a holy anger higher.
What can be purged is not the final act.
Death must surely enter, but no eye
can shape, from the start, that end,
no eye will welcome it.
We ride the daemon's back
to feel the weight of vision,
to balance the thrust of time.

In the eye, clouded by injury,
the texture of maguey is rose,
a caravan of gypsies is at rest.
If we buckle and kneel on the sword's point,
it is to acknowledge the source
      of another strength.
We have come here, under a Basque sign,
to be used up. We will be dragged
into a dark corner, under the Plaza,
to be cut and sent, living,
      into the poorest pots.

SAN DIEGO'S DISPOSSESSION

Clouds fall in San Diego's yard,
finca shape, black liquid
in its pores.
An Aztec urn with cross
struts in its center.
Four pyramidal points surround the cross;
a chevron-hatched phallus holds it erect.
Unnamed, disguised, covered with moss,
the emblem is still a crown of thorns.
San Diego, Saint James,
the Lord's brother,
lightbearer of the mountains,
a pilgrim haunts your open door.
A horsedrawn dickey leaves
to pierce the clouds,
returns, to pierce the silence.
In the New Hampshire woods
there are four nights of moon
and a silence that never leaves.
All fields pray to be inhabited.
The birdmate follows and falls
on his mother-to-be,
in the dark thickets by the road.
This, you hear, is the shriek of love,
the bird people pecking at the water
of joy, the misery of a day's eternal bell.
Ask him, who tolls your height,
for the knowledge
in the wail of our pleasure,
the lilt of our obligation.
It is right that Our Lady of the Field
is figured in stone.
At the height of summer,
when the second eye is figured in its white robes,
Jacob will borrow this pagan wind and rain.
We worship the clarity
of the figure that does not appear.
The clean tree calls us down
to lie in the deep woods,
under the rain that tangles us in green.
The cold light of this tonsure
will possess us, when we return
and fall unseen.

HARMONY'S TRIO

THE CONTINUING CITY: SPIRIT AND BODY

I resist the image of a god,
tipped on a leg, a lonely double blur and egg.
If I accept the direction of the east,
a heavy star will seed me, the light
will lay its solid lines about me;
I step through these to measure what appears.
Soon, it will be difficult to tell
who led me from the derry of jackals
into this habitation of song.
Now, I must accept my descent,
and rise with my stone back set
to diminish the dust hard hills.
I work all things in flesh—
acacia for the veins of my hearth,
another body's blood hide for my bed.
I twirl my pots from the earth's second skin.
Day into day, I walk to the line of my own skin.
Perhaps this city I walk
unfolds from oak roots,
or is unleashed by water
bellied near the deepest rocks;
it may unfurl from crystal or from granite.
I grow into the craft of glass,
and curry all my iron and steel
into the glandular chains of my home.
Where now is the city my eye rules?
How can this body last,
if it must come?
How can the eye rule a body
of constant change?
I measure and control my god's intent
and call it flesh,
the visible intention of sight.
This is the city I consider and compare,
the balance I desire. All else is blindness,
all other speech is numberless.
I have it
that Prophesie shall faile,
and Tongues shall faile,
and Knowledge shall vanish,

and so I try to make a body
contain a certain knowledge,
to free the light to set clear figures in space.
The space around all bodies must be named.
Now, the singer sits to work
this age-old figure into flesh.
Craftsman of the ear and hand,
he acts between the real and all our names;
he finds his image in the act,
his faith in his inability to rub
the god's body
into a bright and lasting city.
I take the earth beneath me
as parchment and intention,
memory and project of all
movement it contains.
I am the dark glass of some other spirit
who will know me, the bone sound
of some other resonant body.
I await my completion in a strange house,
my soul's rags falling in pride from its door.

THE MEASURE

I continue in my gbariye.
All things along my path are clean and white.
I have set out on a flute's quiet wave
in search of my dark love.
Divination and division mark my road;
yet, if I turn from left to right,
I walk the same straight path.
I carry the wine of salt water in my bag
to the crossroads of honey and milk.
I am puffed up and charged with the thought
of my own separation. From light to light,
I continue while the light lasts.
The light rests on my walking pole.
I continue.

If ever you marry, remember,
there is a festival of light
on every island, a garden
where the women gather in white
to turn to the sound of a king's song.
If you ask why the queen is silent,
the dance is ended.
Then only a boy on the cross of roads
can find the blue stone of wisdom,
the lourie feather of love in the flesh.
You ask me to enter the chamber and sing,
groan, inexpressibly, groan, ascend,
descend, leap from the ash of your pillow
to the calm light of your grave.
I am too certain of the measure of these days.
Sojourner and guest, I continue;
I polish new stones from old;
I am at hail's end in the deep wings
of the city; I would return to the feast.
I continue.

I have learned to see a seed as act,
a word as a gift of perfection.
The hand that slips the abundant
seed into the darkness of earth
extends from my body.

I have always wanted to ask—
who speaks, who moves and who returns
when the I is hidden in the paradigm?
I have learned to accept my presence as act,
my act as a placement of time.
I hold now, by my presence,
to have held the first light,
and, in my imperfection,
to have held the vision of my own absence.
This is the one you marry, so lightly.

Each figure, now, twins and untwins us.
We say we can be brought, in white,
to the marriage bed, under a reed's bass,
and settled, limb to counter limb,
with our desert's necessities.
I wait, as always, at the crossroads
to be led into the city.
I desire your double journey.
I ask your name.
I continue.

THE SUNSET'S WIDOW

Ridge hair runny nose
snuff dipped teeth
she loves lilacs and wears
snake garters
     At sunset
she sits on an egg box
spits
at the evening's hesitation
     You find her
in summer quarreling
with the wind but it isn't the wind
alone
that knows her voice

Witness now her voice
       her sign
the serpent cactus spined
and smooth as oil
caressing her neck

Witness now
the pattern of her body's lines
the curves and undulations
the sweep
   toward the hard case
     of her garters
     the hard eyes
that would be there
that would hold you
    as still as a bird

Root lovely woman
the love of a bitter root
tea fangs and shells
a bitter egg
  that will not hatch
all serpentine and green
but the lilac but the lilac
determines here
the rough cast and bitter root
of everything of everything
but the witness

But the witness
determines
the rough cast
and bitter root
    of the evening's hesitation
    spit   an egg box
    snake garters at sunset
    weary lilacs
    snuff   snot   and the line
    dying
        at the crown
            of the head.

THE BODY

(man)

1

All day we charge
the sun toward its tomb.
I canter after you,
a buck myself,
placed by your coat and flaming hair,
in the green darkness around us.
Up ahead, we hear
the crack and spit of rifles,
the momentary whistle of trees,
a branch split
and then the silence.
All these antlered heads we track
sprout like bushes or ferns,
trying pitifully
to withdraw into the earth,
hoping their silence and stillness
will take us past and off
to an enemy,
moving fiercely, tangled
in the labyrinth
we make by moving ourselves.
With the rifle, you lead;
I follow with a knife,
feeling myself too well-armed,
shy at its touch
against my leg.
We stalk these hills
for my childhood,
and the solitary, crooked cook
who could not kill,
our penance to prove
that nothing is right
but blood and the memory of it.
So I know
there will be no return
until we have drained the sun
of all its light.
Still, smoothly,

you push ahead, and circle,
and move as though the measure
had been set by God,
or some forgotten brother.
Perhaps it is memory.
Perhaps it is this presence
of the palpable deer
within me,
the breath, heart level and unafraid,
eyes the light of a movement,
the search
that will not end in death alone.
We wait in the silence now
for the one that has chosen us.
This, now, is the limit of our movement,
a point in the restless plane
of bushes and ferns,
dead trees, one body
moving toward this closed space.
And this is the point
of a remembered space,
focus of feeling,
focus of the steps concerned,
the mask with which I dress your face.
With all these poles
and definitions set,
I see you settle in the darkness.
Alone, I listen
for an unfamiliar step,
and know it may not come.

(woman)
2

Pinched, at the peak of summer,
between two rivers,
I stroll to this corner
and wait for you.
You know the telling time,
and come just at the right time,
walking from the other shore,

along 125th,
your robe so white
the lights defile it,
your hair hidden under a veil,
a Magdalene, or conjure woman,
smelling of snake root oil.
No one knows from where you come,
but we hear your first step,
feel the deliberate sternness of your dress,
moving toward us.
No one would take your corner.
No one would move within that field,
at that hour; no one
would move from it.
You come,
and even the snap of dice subsides;
cars, bars, lights and we ourselves
move without sound.
We pass and pass,
as though we were linked to you,
linked to your voice,
linked again to the rhythm of your body,
the set and ground of all movement,
the point and measure
that serve this source and ground
on which you move.
Say I wait and come here,
bearing the weight of a city
without measure,
to nestle under your left eye.
Say I snuggle here
in the cuddle of a crowd
you caress and scorn,
trying to measure its light,
trying to determine what form I take,
or lose, in its brief regard.
Often, you descend the box,
and chalk a circle and cross,
another eye, at our feet.
You chant and scream in another tongue,
and stop and listen for echoes.
You know we will not speak.
You need the tense presence of our bodies

to filter the sound,
to filter the light,
to touch and recognize
the achievement of your voice
—that other god,
who takes the deliberate measure
of a city that will not fit.
Night after night,
you stand at this corner,
and beg us not to be afraid.
You turn and step along a line
in each direction,
as though you were dancing,
as though the dance
would establish some living point,
design a body,
rising at that point
to enter and shake you
until you were changed
or our eyes admitted it so.
This is a gathering of Baptist boys,
Rollers, witches and saints,
a choir of the fallen
who have not been released,
who would grovel under the lash
of your tongue,
to return, in the heat of your eye,
to a presence we may not remember,
but know.

(the man's soul)

3

Fishermen out there in the dark—O you
Who rake the waves or chase their wake—
Weave for him a shadow out of your laughter
For a dumb child to hide his nakedness . . .
    Christopher Okigbo, *Lament of the Drums, III*

Long before dawn,
the fishermen wake
in the season,
take their three-tiered
lunch buckets,
their straw hats
and quexquémetls,
and wind,
barefoot and secretive,
through the maze and stillness
of this rough-grained town,
down to the lake.
All night
I have lain,
crutched in an old cockleshell,
crushing sand crabs
that dart after the searchlight
(their hint of sun),
listening to the late serenades
tuck the lovers into yesterday.
I watch the fishermen
take their small boats,
load them with nets
and push off for the deep
part of the lake.
Slowly, one by one,
they row away, and move
until they are strung,
dark and silent birds,
nesting on the surface.

At this hour,
the water, a spider's web, accepts
their movement and their stillness.
The cave welcomes the boy
with the right amount of light.
I return and turn to them
again each morning,
and wait for that moment
between the movement and the stillness
when the men, stretched out,
seem to be praying,
listening and testing the depths
for a murmur of discontent.
They do not turn to each other,
or call, or gesture,
but rise, one body awaking,
and drop their nets,
looking into the water,
listening again,
taking the task step by step,
fixing the morning
with these real movements and signs.
Each day, the movements
are only shadows of themselves.
The men, clothed just so,
are memories of themselves.
They take the water, and return,
and do not know, or care,
that I watch and work
my own order.
They have their own,
and float back into the light,
to wind their ropes around their waists,
and dance their nets and fish
into the hungry arms of the women,
come from the maze and stillness of the town,
waiting on the shore.

(the woman's soul)

4

You sit on your stool,
at the head of your rug,
dip, palm and rake these beans,
and pick the stones and burrs away.
With the right touch of sun,
the right angle and measure
of your touch, these brown
and melancholy sprouts
are cowries, shells,
sea-tinged pearls,
the infinite eye of God.
At dawn,
you clap your children
into dun brown coats,
as though you would disguise them,
and send them along the roads,
over moss-covered fences,
into any corner and cave
that will yield a bean.
You wash your rug
and brush your dress,
and shake and brush your hair.
You move in the early light,
singing, and plotting the place
where each bean will fall,
each color lit by the space
it will take,
each space lit
by the presence of the bean.
You enter the market
and sit erect, waiting
for the boys' return,
the brown and threadbare sacks
to be set just at your right hand.
This is little enough to start
your singing again,
little enough to have you call
and welcome the timid foragers
close to the circle and sparkle

of your rug, the plucked seeds,
stars spread out and radiant.
Pulled from the earth,
they show their signs,
until you pinch
their vestiges of navels.
Cleaned now,
they take their final form
upon your rug,
dipped, palmed and raked into light,
their skins already beginning to wrinkle
and break away from your love.

TWENTY-TWO TREMBLINGS
OF THE POSTULANT

(Improvisations Surrounding the Body)

I

1 (arm)

Candles, ribbons and a cross
                gaud my sash and tux.
My derby and white gloves
stand erect over my coffin.
This music greets death,
           the winking, prancing lid
that lies
          still with longing
              for a bone that has flared,
              an embryo with the power to appear.

2 (forearm)

Between
        the hand and these long bones,
eight bones,
as small as covenant stones,
lie and turn about.
Articulate grip,
such force,
           a god's delicate disguise,
alters the marks of the altar stones.

3 (shoulder blade)

Companioned pity, doubt's
double contradiction
      reveal
the body's incisive intent.
Cut and placed just so,
they would seem to turn
         from sun to moonrise,
each state and figure carefully defined.
Caulicle scribes of heaven's notice,
they graph love's
       irradiant positions.
Under the head's strict account,
the body's lost arc and arch
count the platelets in love's force.

4 (fingers)
for Albert Ayler

Patron of a dap,
      a dapper sound,
let us here recall
breath,
presence
and desire.
Witch moss listens for the elephant horn,
the dirge of imprisoned light.
Darkness charges your bell's light;
its emptiness endures
       in your free light,
point without closure,
space without beginning.
Your fingers must endure
   the astringent eyes
     your horn wears.

IV
5 (thigh)

To him who has not killed
it is forbidden to drink
                the virgin's beer.
Sun and son of the thigh mark
must press the distance
            deeper into the spirit's grip.
                You sail,
                shorts slit so high
                the cloth billows
                and rides
                around your waist.
This stadium veils the paradigm of the race;
the wood obscures the declension of the hunt.
Your tempered thighs, contesting air,
            unfurl love's amber presence.

6 (tibia)

Your father guards the story in a cedar box:
a vulture's tracks, fish bones, a cattle head,
discarded mat, sheared pot, the forgotten
dispositions that empowered your music.

The dry north calls the whistle and whisper
of a darkened cave from Muslim mouths.
You have returned with your bleached, marrowed
bone, home of the god's throat,
            embedded
in the flute certainty,
            in the midnight
of the cave's red, comforting leaves.

I
7 (foot)

Even at night,
a trace of sunlight hangs in the east.
Air creates an immobile, blue canticle.
The seagulls' incapable wings remain
"merely an unwithering tumble,
a chute of angels fallen
by a sheer delight in their weight."
You set out in the delight of a fall.
Flight's image defines
      the conjunction of your besieged foot
with the zodiac of a timeless god's
                   weightless grief.

8 (lower jaw)

Dressed and belled in perfect order,
we arrive under the tomb sound,
the antiphonal knock of the smith.
We have enshrined the speaker's ninth hour,
harmony's impulse, in visible acts.
The knife's deep exaltation settles
the mouth's thirty-two degrees, exults
the votive articulation of the unspeakable.
Our stripped gifts of measure and control
begin the descent of the shuddering,
                  communal jaw.

V
9 (toes)

Disguised,
I walk by night
and listen for the rain.
It slips upon and shakes
these blue white nameless wings.
The rumor of roses, gossip of foxgloves
remember death's cause.
Night refuses to fit the cluster
of cobblestones, bees' lamps,
a woman's scented and magic pot.
The rain in the bird's wings, the antelope's
certain hoofbeat raise the dead
                    at the moment of rest.
I must remember to discover
the unfamiliar terrain of my shadow,
the donu bird's scale in my toes
                    on the ground.

10 (anus)

Why should you come,
            with your voice filled
                    with the morning's bright oranges,
to be saddled and hiccuped into pleasure?
Love dresses, in this room,
            in the wrong color.
            I light
cold water in a porcelain bowl
to cover the swiveled space
            the barbed god left us.
Five yams, five kola nuts, two logs
            of firewood from the ita tree.
Junior wife of the road,
I have sponged holiness
            into the room's extended body.
Now you must touch my deepest disguise
            and pray for an uncorrupted star,
                    the light of an uncontaminated ship.

I
11 (nose)

The dignity in beaten maize abrades the nose.
Brute heat rises, weed strong, above the lake's decline.
Shellfish embrace the moon disc on the shore.
Our memory of passage lodges in a goatskin,
                              lashed to a rock.
Night breathes in a crystal purity
and in the sleep of comfort in burnt cactus.
We descend,
              from the sun's point,
on the red liquid of exchange.
The cocoa smell of cayenne fills the desert
and assures us that the cut will heal,
the scar will disappear.

12 (mouth)

Six o'clock.
Blanketed and muffled,
we circle the reclining forest,
through the morning's guard
of drooping banana leaves,
cacti, clumps of grass,
              dead rhododendrons.
                 Conjure
a cedar stump for your hand
and a likeness in a cradled, scented body.
If silence is the forest's majestic word,
the name it invokes at dawn,
the mouth must be bridled,
until the tree has understood
       its canon death in the carver's song.

I

13 (hair, head and neck)

Near dawn, she purls through the brush
to appear, sibilant and serene, at the elder's blueberry stream.
Midwife of God's unbroken hour,
she cuts his morning body for the stars,
lotus, donu bird, calabash and stolen seed,
all the fiction of his craft and command.
Her plaited, pearled hair now measures
danger's intervals in a heron dream,
the reptilian night, in a virginal return,
a death without end.
She has taught me the limits of contemplation
and the way a bone,
     though it be taken from the truest cross,
                   decays.
I have it from her conch in the water's web:
high tribulation attends every celebratory bell.
I know now, my woman will bell down berries
at the water's edge, to press a devotee's
uneasiness into my traveling bones.

14 (chest)

I know this country by the myth of the rose,
those linden tenors, lilting swords, unruly loves,
larcenous runts who rise from the mist at the peak
of an insurmountable passion.
I have been given the book of a peasant heart
and the cave for a passion other than my own.
I would acknowledge my journey
               down
         the decent path
            of tenure, here to the grammar of being,
standing-in-itself, arising, enduring,
the radical exegesis of the false myth of existence.
Sausage dark blood piques my thirst again
     for the intemperate sword and jackboot love
     my body holds for itself.

15 (stomach)

I would have you an unblemished bell,
an angular assertive god, text for the perfect
singer in the perfect grove
                                    or carve you
in ebony or sandstone, a toucan perched in an ebony
bowl in a corner of this room.
You understand the danger of being stripped
of totem and amulet, the bliss of being cold
to a god's stroke and set, untangled,
darkened in wisdom, in the direction of a self
                                    you may never reach.
A migratory man, licked by the serpent,
you dug your life from under withered baobab,
became your own, a seventh, son.
I turn and turn.   You remain.
You have taken your insatiable appetite
away from the limits of our love.

16 (ear)

Pagan by birth, you arrange your route by spring.
You bring your eastern, skitterish saw to cradle us into night.
For days, you boil us in hymns,
stopping only to admire your wife, in white
from heel to head, stutter into tongues
                                    or stagger into dance.
We raise you into prophecy and offer you
this house, the left-over moments of ecstasy,
the right to pierce our hearts with your fluent saw.
All night, the women clasp the serpent's sting
and reel uncertainly after your melodies,
into your wife's design or into inventive glosses
upon your meager lexicon.
                                    This, too,
is the watch for that star's spin, the seed's turn.
This, too, is the ear open
to the accumulation that begins our death.
Strange, how you, having taught an element to sing,

come unmasked, riding the morning into night,
invoking the music which binds you to this place,
able to distinguish what little can be spoken,
or what space the silence leaves
                                to redeem our souls.

                        IV

                  17 (sides)

        Come sunset you can bet
        like a moth at a flame
        old Blind Man will be here
        cue caught up in his crotch
        cup of Mr. Boston cuddled
        under a corner of the table

        take a nickel more
        if you can run six
        before he get a line
        got such an eggplucking touch
        young men close their eyes and sleep
        stand at his side   and learn

        money down mouth back
        come light   beef up
        hey   take a nickel on a run
        who want to shoot the Blind Man one

        buy a drink   you will.

18 (spinal column)

High in the wind,
Chinese gongs quiver in the night.
                    It is winter.
All day I play with your fig wine vision
and tamper with the tricks love has taught my tongue.
Here, I have a moment to construct the path you set me.
I am at bells' end,
buckled in the shift you spur.
I have truckled to the arks and bright beds
of virgins who could not be clear.
Let me tell you of the wickedness of spring
and the giddy danger of unthreading a maze.
I know, and regret, the moon's embrace
of the straightbacked, nubile sun.

I

19 (kidneys)

In time,
in tune and omen rich,
I spin about my body,
at ease with my sabbath temper.

I know there is a mark
upon the man who only knows
a penitent's shiver at a Joshua tree,
whose only peace is

intoxicated stillness,
or the breath of holiness
that comes when evil, faced,
has been denied.

But what can we deny,
when each body falls,
plump with his father's gifts,
into this body already rich

with the god's gifts?
Your shepherds now shiver under these bells.
They stamp about our feet
and pinch their fingers at our mouths.

Disguised,
I rise, under your eyes, from dung,
to begin my trembling.
My eyes remember

the goat's quiver,
my purity's star-bound blood,
the liver-laden word
in its moon cold silence.

Redeemed, I keep
longing's mark on my body.
Just once I turn away,
finding these fathers' gifts

too much to bear.

20 (clavicle)

My dancing master of the gold bead,
I see you trouble the waters
        between that moment of light
and the star's darkness.
                        Doubled
in your body, you wake; you twist,
then lurch, your body into motion.
Played upon by love's one breath,
you mount your antelope, the horse
who releases the cull bone god in you.
You annoint me the coffin's scribe.
A second birth folds us head to head.
Death doubles us to ride
        earth's sunken ark
toward a second and hazardous light.

Master, remember it was you,
discontent with your own imitation,
who frayed and made these bones delicate
    by bathing them in time.

V
21 (back of the hand)

Light,
night's unladen image
in your wedding dress, the thin line
erasing heaven's darkness,
staunches me in its shadow.

All night,
I feel you smack my cheek
and wake me to the thunder
of your breathing,
        a mother's moan,
a bride's clamor for rain.

Surgical,
you could part my body
along earth's axes; spirit me
among your father's oaths and altars.

I belong to the figure
   of the rain
you coil with your hand,
the stones that find
their places only at your touch.

If I awake, with you,
in darkness, it is the clean
incision of your love
that calls the light to dance,
just out of reach,
    on earth that rises
       clearly
without the press of your hand.

22 (eye)

Ecstatic, full,
and still half-blind,
I see you clear your body
of its scars.
        Astonished
by the magic of my name,
I name your scars, the angry cuts
stitched and hidden from yourself.
How shall we measure these bleached bones?
How shall we disregard the curry of a prophetic fox?
All peace is stolen,
    a disfigured rite,
nourished by your scars and breathless denials.
Those others now know my name.
Yet how can we possess
what you yourself have lost?
We own no land,
no love, no art, no death.
We walk among these signs of your
dispossession
and hear you say you passed this way,
like this,
        and it was right.

      (The last two bars are tacit.)

MACINTYRE, THE CAPTAIN AND THE SAINTS

A northern light at midnight
wakes the bronze upon the hill.
The crowned clock sits on the tower
in a gable's eye. And I,
a serpent of the east,
unwind at Lothian Road.
This
has been my dungeon,
through the day
and through the evening.
But now, at night,
my walls are glass;
they bubble under
the heathenish touch,
till they are forest and sea,
till they become one holy
coracle, by which
I am coiled to the house.
I live by the darkness
of these other walls.
I turn on the cross
of the house that lights them.
Again I wake in the royal burgh
                              of Edinburgh.
I turn in the Castle's deep,
and go where the city's life
lies on the market.
A watch and an ivory cane handle
lead me over His Majesty's bridge.
Saint Giles, the Law, High Street—
I salute High John.
I go into the close
above Waverley, below
the jolly *Scotsman*.
This is my castle
of hotpies and rest,
one-half an ale.
The keeper keeps a tap
upon my nights;
I keep the morning.

I call great John O'Groats,
the Hill O' Many Stanes,
Gray Cairns of Camster,
Craigievar,
the Temple of Carinish,
Elgin Cathedral,
Lantern of the North,
victim of Wolf of Badenoch.
I call my David
for the rights of trading;
I posit my burghs—
Dunfermline, Perth, Stirling
and Aberdeen.
What is my eye
but the chief's eye?
What shield but his name?
Yet I am not Pict by Scot;
great Kenneth is not my king.
I take my concepts and my kin
from desert waters.
I have belted my bones
with ritual invocations.
Now, should I turn from this,
and run from my rose garden
and my kilt
            into another darkness?
No, I think that I shall stand,
and stand called to see
who is the *I* of this constellation,
what is the shape of this life.

> And on a birlan edge I see
Wee Scotland squattin like a flea . . . <

I see you now,
and I would dizen
and divvy your birlan eyes
to protect me.
Saint Christopher, welcome
to my castle keep,
my night of stars
and desert memories,
your own *planctus*
in the boat of history.

45

> Drums in the Walligate, pipes in the air,
Come and hear the cryin o the Fair . . .

Drums in the Walligate, pipes in the air,
The wallopan thistle is ill to bear . . .   <

I know ye dinna ken my sound,
so I'll speak to you
in the sweetness your tongue belies.

I'll accept your grace.

And I'll accept your cup.

Ale in the close.

Whiskey to wash away
the stain of the rose.

We drink away the sugar on our tongues,
and take the Mound.
The school of doctors waits in darkness.
A morning coat with keys,
a gentleman, with bones draped blue
with mourning, waits in the thistle air.
His blue is cut by one small key.
I think of this,
and wonder what a key may be.
I think of locks I cannot open,
locks I cannot lock.
Wee Scotland still is a howling babe
in the breech this key will miss.

Are you happy on the Mound?
*The Equivalents set that tail‡
on the gardens.
We are still, in this high air,
mixed by money and God.

I know that.

You cannot know it;
you can only see.

This Mound is weary
with the thought—
an Irishman, a Pictish king
brought Jesus to us.
Yet even still, I think
I hold him dear—
*a royal man, a scholar,
abstemious and gifted
with a second sight,
and fine hand,
"none of your St. Maluag
of Lismore, or your drybones
of Pictland."‡
If we wait,
we'll hear that first James
promise God to see that
*"the key keep the castle
and the bracken bush the kye."‡

It was St. Ninian who brought the key.

You do not even know.

But I do belong.
Look here,
I have my tartan
on the Princes street.
My name is MacIntyre.

You show your purpose.

I'm searching for my purpose,
and it cannot be in blood
or in Highland drafts of praise.

The light is still,
and time is a movement into light.
In the moonlight, here on Princes Street,
I stare into the colors of my Celtic name.

If you plumed yourself in this,
I'd break your hips,
I'd sever your shoulders.
I taught you more than this.

Yes, Captain, I am sure I learned
my lessons well from you.

                    Then?

Then, I leave you.
Oxford tames what London teaches.
My Danquah learns from Hobhouse
what he could see at home.

                    Before he came,
                    I said this.

You called the proverbs
ethics of a savage people.

                    I knew no other words.
                    I learned.

To speak more carefully.

                    Yes. And more simply.
                    There follow:
                    Ashanti,
                    Religion and Art in Ashanti,
                    Akan-Ashanti Folktales.
                    These things are true.

They were true then.

                    I know that. I quote,
                  > I have taken every opportunity,
                    while gathering material from my
                    Ashanti friends, to impress upon
                    them strongly that our culture,
                    our ideas, arts, customs, dress,
                    should not be embraced by them
                    to the entire exclusion and ex-
                    tinction of what is good, just
                    and praiseworthy in their ancient
                    national institutions. <
                    The hope is in the sunsum.
                    I suffered for this.

Half mad from teaching
a tongue to Great Stuart Street,
I was on my island.

You condemn me, too.

You were the Scot
who took the cause
from New Town to Kumasi.

I took my life there.
I saw my kindred spirits there.
I returned, puff-hot in tweeds,
a fuller man.

I suppose I will return
myself, puff-hot in tartan,
a better man.

A fuller man.
Haven't you learned anything?
The good is all of us.
It is never lost.
If you are better,
it is not from the perfection
of virtue, but the perception
of virtue, the acceptance
of the okara.

You, in this city of daggers
and shields, instruct me?

The sunsum teaches.

> Nae man can ken his hert until
the tide o life uncovers it . . . <

The sunsum teaches this.

I am the angel of sunsum,
the breath of rain that fights
to fill the foam with mercy.
If the god does not appear,

49

then we must imagine him
in blue, or in the dun of earth,
or in the red of bronze, imagine
him wreathed with his own shrieking hands.
Now, I turn from my tartan, Captain,
along St. David Street.

>**As Mr. David Hume's circumstances improved he enlarged
his mode of living, and instead of the roasted hen and minced
collops, and a bottle of punch, he gave both elegant dinners
and suppers, and the best claret, and, which was best of all,
he furnished the entertainment with the most instructive
and pleasing conversation . . .**

>*Lord Monboddo says
the man died—
confessing not his sins
but his Scotticisms.*

He still was a gentle man,
a daemon of good sense,
whose good sense disturbs.
If, in the light that carries
us along this road, we could
see him, startled by a piece
of woolen cloth, lord of astronomy,
savior of ethics, we could place
herring and hides in the deep fissures
of our souls. He is indeed dead,
but much of him still lives among us.
I believe that there is cause
to see him yet.

So it is night in our royal burgh.
The father of Common Sense has been let out.
The boys from the country gather
in the hill mists. I repeat:
Robertson, John Home, Bannatine,
Alexander Carlyle and Adam Smith
and Ferguson, Lord Elibank, Doctors
Jardine and Blair.
    Who is this
who walks with a key in hand?

Oh, then, good St. David,
by whose authority do you walk?

> None . . . can go beyond experience,
   or establish any principles
   which are not founded
                    on that authority. <

        You are here.

I do perceive myself.

Well, I pucker and refuse
to enter that clam of memory.

        Enter, if you believe in the imagination.

Your memory and your belief
lead me away from that.

        I struggled with belief,
        not under your saints' bells,
        but here under the dissolving
        assurance of my skin.

                This is from Johnny Knox,
                Geneva bound.
            ***Those who are saved
                have certainty of it
                in their faith, that
                they are God's elect.***

        I glorify God,
        but I will not toll
        man's corruption.

        This is needless.

                *It is the visible body
                under the head of Christ.*
                Do you deny it?
                Do you deny a nation
                can believe that God
                        will provide?

> Let men be persuaded . . . that there is nothing
in any object, considered in itself, which can
afford us a reason for drawing a conclusion
beyond it . . . <

   *The doctors at Aberdeen
   refused to subscribe.
   Lady Huntly lay in state
   at the head of a brave funeral.
   They had the town's haill
   ordinance for ane good night,
   and the Marquis had taken
   his household and children
   back to the country in high
   melancholie. Wine and sweetmeats
   were offered to the Covenant
   embassy, and refused while
   the Covenant was unsigned.
   The provost and the baillies
   gave the banquet to the poor.‡

/It is for God to judge whether the Least shadow
or footsteps of freedom can be discovered in this
assembly./

  > The only defect of our senses is
  that they give us disproportionate
  images of things. <

   *Spring corn and oats and barley
   were all we had.
   He gave us Easter and other
   movable feasts, the shape
   of the tonsure. By Margaret's
   and Malcolm's time, we had
   lost Iona; our kings were buried
   in a Benedictine abbey
        in Dunfermline.‡

You hold me responsible for what was done?
I recorded this.

52

/God hath a people here fearing his name, though deceived./

And all my kin Barbadoed from the house.
I return, or do I return?
Do I hear the reason in St. David's voice?
Do I now enter myself most intimately,
and find myself able to entertain
a diffidence and modesty in all my decisions?
Do I remember the special light St. David gave?

> If reason determined us, it would proceed
upon that principle, that instances,
of which we have had no experience, must
resemble those of which we have had
experience, and that the course of nature
continues always uniformly the same. <

Oh, then, let our lives be bled
upon the roses of our trimmed days.
This is no' comfort, but a spike
in the tongue, a gate against
true memory.
> And yet, I dinna haud the warld's end
in my heid. <

Old Saint, I know you know
the *Gude and Godlie Ballads*.
Just in faith, the head
is redeemed by the head.
I twit you on the world's end.
The text excludes you as a saint.
You have no hiding place,
no bawdy of perfection.
The body will not be quickened
on your tongue. If there is
a word to speak, and one author
stands above it, how could your body
be revealed upon these stones?
I read you as revealed in your own text,
but read you in a feminine text now dead.
If the witches presume,
Saint David puckers.
What can be known, appears;

what appears, lies among us.
Then the offensive witches
must go down in their own glory,
and the king must search the basements.
I have heard it was said from the scaffold
that
**God hath laid engagements on Scotland:
We are tyed by covenants to religion
and reformation; those who were then
unborn are engaged to it, in our baptism
we are engag'd to it; and it passeth
the power of all Magistrates under heaven
to absolve a man from the oath of God.**

                                    I know,
                    > The thocht o Christ and Calvary
                      Aye liddenin in my heid;
                      And aa the dour provincial thocht
                      That merks the Scottish breed
                       —These are the thistle's characters. <

No, not the thistle's alone.

        I only understand
          *quantity and number
           matter of fact and existence
           all else
                is sophistry and illusion.*

           All else is the king's realm,
           and the king's realm is
                      spirit and body,
                  dying and being born,
                  living on reason's unadorned shores.
           Why do you quibble?
           Why have you sent me with cap
           and compass to confirm these facts?

Can the facts grow from vision?
Can a new star arise to figure
           a new constellation?

> I find myself involv'd in such a labyrinth,
that, I must confess, I neither know how
to correct my former opinions, nor how
to render them consistent. < Yes, it is
sufficient reason for diffidence and modesty.

> Darkness is wi us aa the time, and Licht
But veesits pairt o us, the wee-est pairt
Frae time to time on a short day atween
twa nichts. <

**Deum de Deo, lumen de lumine,
Deum vero de vero Deo, genitum,
non factum . . . **

Wright, would you hurt me in this way?

Saint Christopher,
poet to poet and soul to soul,
we insist on our darkness;
yet we may be wrong.
There may be more light
in David's perpetual twilight
than in our hidden hope for light.
We live between the two nights.
We await the light.
A game of billiards may be
all our affirmation of hope,
crowned, in our anguish, belief.
Or do we find we have two bodies
—a yellow seed split open by the sun,
a blue stem caressed by moonlight—
and each embodied by a reason?
Though I have never been your king,
you give me cain and conveth.
I would not burn your Cardinalle's town.
Saint David, believe
I know the debility of my own assurance.
Captain,
I have met you in the gulf.
Here, in my lean years, I have risen to say:
God is not *propter quid*, but *quia*,
a reasoning in an empty vessel.

We know, or think we feel,
our bodies calm upon the wave
which has its own design.
Bird-boned, we contend with the fire
        within us.
What is our intention but the fire
        within us,
or the description of a body
clarified by a wind?
We may live through the bone blaze
of our bodies and know only
how to shiver each bone from its scaffold,
each cell from its surface.
Surely, it is pain to reveal
the indifference of God's substance,
to acknowledge we are sufficient
only in his grace. Singular,
we prove and construct what we may
                only know.
The years rigor and steep
these questions in your faces;
I read the night's unhurried return there;
you temper your return to me.
Your air can promise me nothing
but the thistle's sense of the spirit.
The cuckoo in the Hebrides would only bind
my blue wings. I know the air as gold,
the shell of an egg; I marry in the moon's seed.
I rehearse all reasons to be false to you.
Now the night covers my serpent skin.
I slip away.
Your night remains.
You ask for assurance;
it comes; as a star falls,

hart for the hind of our shadowed world.
I crown and sceptre you with your blood
burden, and hear the echo of my own.

LOVE'S DOZEN

THE RITUAL TUNING

Now I will enter the house of affliction.

King carry me above myself in death.
Awake to the king of all,
I come, regal in my purpose,
out of the heated darkness.
Tune me only now;
I tune myself to your love
and your many-eyed longings,
to your deepest look into your life.

I am the contradictions that you make me.
Scaled, I climb your trees.
I lay my eggs, one by one,
and suckle them.
And in my sign I raise
the bright seed of my spirit.

I am two heads in one,
two lives in one.
I end my life in a double vision.
When I am eaten, you pass
this double deed among yourselves.

Love is to enter another's house
a creature coined from vision's deepest pain.

Here, creature of heaven,
I surround you with my sign,
and look upon your marriage bed,
and look upon your death.

LOVE IN THE WATER, LOVE IN THE STONE

Faithful bean lady of the plantain,
your tubular beads surround my voice.
You bring me a berry song so old
I hug the silences. You
embrace the silence and the clear light
on the track of your quest, to here.
I see now in that light myself
into the tangle of the river's bottom.

Knee-deep in another's bliss,
I wake and find myself a stone
                              at your lover's feet.
Then stone upon stone,
I rise into another's fire.
I touch your palm oil flesh
to light me from my cave.
And, if I rise, under your thunder,
into rain, I praise your touch.

Now, life-long a laterite,
a rain of beads, palm kernel oil
stipulate my clipped time.
The earth weaves eight gold bridal veils
to cast into the sea. The moon
is up at noon to catch me naked,
drunk and dancing with a ram.
I use the loom of seasons so;
I abuse myself.
And, even if I leave you,
I marry your worship in my wife's voice.

I begin the decline of having you
                              close;
your memories feed me.
These are my intolerable survivals.
And so I take my love's journey
from the language of your needs.
I mount my woman's earth smell
in the shadows of your ageless eyes.
I crawl to the altar of your thunderstones
and bleed for the bride whose blood
will fill my name.

LOVE IN THE IRON AND LOOM

Double the earth in northern light;
double the west in water.
Twin me in iron and weaving.
Binu, Lébé, my male hand
knows my woman's hardness.
I am the twin of my head, the twin of my hand.
Woven into cloth,
I slither from the dance a mask.
I am a dance in mask.
Who will answer the figure of the dance?
Who will unmask the twin at my heart?
My water shape in stone has a grip
                              upon the earth.
My river has a line around the star.
Shuttle and hammer, my life coheres.
My axe is the altar stone,
the loom of your love.
I know you as my cold light,
and as my dying light,
and as the barking star I ride
through love's light.
My lord's light is the deep pit
                    of my marriage bed,
the song of my sign within the dance.
Weep, weep, weep.
Brother mask, you leap
to double me from myself.
I am broken.
I am finished.
I weep for the twist of my craft
in the green river of my god's love.

LOVE AS HEAVEN'S NOSTALGIA

Rhine moonstone, light
of the devastated world,
I could name your nobleness
in minerals and stars,
or in the light's courage.
Yet in my ear the ages linger.
I know your passion for a melody,
your nostalgia for heaven.
I wait, under your touch,
for the vision of your governing.
Sisters, I will awaken in myself
your melodic temper.
Strange how my life runs down to reason
in the memory of a bright daughter;
I am at the gate of a lost life;
I am at the door of my own harmony.
And you, delivered from this world,
summon my purified soul to sit
in its nature with the stars.

ANAGNORISIS

Through blood
and into blood
my spirit calls.
You sit at my head
and weave my power.
Queen, I do not do as you
and deal in deaths.
I have no power to make
that male power crawl to my knees.
Yet I speak and am your seer,
chaste lover and your bridge
                from the dead one's
blackened space
to the white sun of your prayer,
the red demon of your mother love.

You took the crescent moon and named me.
You bought my axe and sent me
through the desert of my southern dreams.
Clearly, in my sign,
I love
your overburdened body.
I love you
as the black chapel
                of my penitence.
I love your forest's touch
in winter's memory.
Now, I grapple your deeds to my tongue.
And out of your woman's common eye,
I take my son's pursuit
of the days he must live
                        to recall.

TRANSCENDENT NIGHT

Your feather hands
are love's nest in winter,
and yet I fly,
or do I dream I fly.
And I wóuld fly
to nestle near your child's lake,
to press my needs upon your feather hands.
There at the lake,
in the shadow of the celt
I find there,
I dance in your spine's darkness;
I clothe you in your spirit's darkness
and in your body's darkness.
I awake to the light of your total darkness.
I keep, for my constant spring,
your feather hands upon my eyes.
My eyes will always take
the dark path to your heart.
My heart will drink its light
from the only heavy hands
                              you offer me.
Death of the dark. Death of the light.
I live in my spirit's web of love's
                              transcendent night.

LOVE IN THE WEATHER'S BELLS

Snow hurries
the strawberries
from the bush.
Star-wet water rides
you into summer,
into my autumn.
Your cactus hands
are at my heart again.
Lady, I court
my dream of you
in lilies and in rain.
I vest myself
in your oldest memory
and in my oldest need.
And in my passion
you are the deepest blue
of the oldest rose.
Star circle me an axe.
I cannot cut myself
from any of your emblems.
It will soon be cold here,
and dark here;
the grass will lie flat
to search for its spring head.
I will bow again
in the winter of your eyes.
If there is music,
it will be the weather's bells
to call me to the abandoned chapel
of your simple body.

THE CROSSES MEET

Patiently, I set your seat
in cedar and a bit of gold,
and by its arms
I cross our lives.
And then I turn your body
toward the wind,
my path from worship
to certainty.
Now, may I house
my woman's meaning
in angels and in stone.
I hold this pagan three-in-one
under your lips
and under your last sign.
Could, now, I trade
your daemons for her body,
I would cut the hardwood
of your seat to peace.
But can you hear me
when I press my preservation
at her knees,
and leap from the tangle
of your seated cross
to the bell of my own voice
at her worship?
You hear me
as I walk from dark
                  to dawn
to save you.
And so I do save you
when my voice
is at her service.
I serve and preserve myself
in her grace.
I sit her on the tangled
stool of grace.
I take her voice alone
to rule in my politic body.

At last your crosses meet
in the love above love,
in the word that spells itself
                              in silence,
and I am the carpenter
of your new spirit
that speaks to hear itself
                              in stone.

LOVE PLUMBS TO THE CENTER
OF THE EARTH

1

I will live with winter
and its sorrows.
Here, the earth folds its blanket
                    at noon.
The eastern crown appears,
disappears,
appears
to lie in pine
on the west ridge.
Some light has been lost;
a stillness has been betrayed.

I seem to feel your body
shake that stillness through the deep
water which separates us now.
Your husband, my father,
plumb of the earth
from our air to his,
lies in the silence of water
we gave to him.

You say you sit at night afraid,
and count the gifts you carried
                    to his bed.
I know that they contain
this fear of the winter's sorrows,
this offense of being left above
the deep water
to pluck this plumb string
for a tremor of love.
But it isn't the melody of loss
you have in your moon bucket,
nor the certainty of a line
                    to your own pain.
The clamor that rides this line
unhinges sorrow,
unburdens its beatific companions.

This single string,
a heart's flow,
is a music of possession.
And so you twin me
in the plain song of survival,
in the deep chant of winter
and its own sun.
Our balance is that body
and the sun extended
                              from our grief.

2

Today,
nine days
after the hunters have gone,
a buck walks from the forest,
and nuzzles at my snow-heavy trees.
I crown him king of the noon,
and watch the light drip from his coat.
In these woods,
his light is a darkness,
an accommodation with winter
and its mid-day shroud.
And, if at night, the moon
holds down its spoon cup,
he will be fed by light
that holds the darkness in it.
His body is the plumb line
the stars shake upon our earth.
Now, will I dare to follow
and to name his steps
through every darkness of our earth,
or shall I turn from that light
to my own winter's light?

3

Left. Right.
Turn. And counterturn.
I would have my foundation stone.
And so I carefully turn my words
about your longing.
Soil, water, root and seed,
the pin of light on which your love
will ride to air finds and turns
in the heart of each of its possessions.
You own me in the grief
                    you will not bear,
and in the act you will not name.
You crown my darkness in your silence,
and you crown me king of my engendered light.
If I possess a seat to rule,
I rule love's coming and the taut
sound of my father's voice in you.
Voices of that deep water stretch
into heaven on a thin line filled
with all we do not possess.

THE UNWEDDING OF THE MAGDALENE
OF THE VINE

Down, on your bare feet,
with a wicker basket of tomatoes,
you come to the courtyard of blue roses,
rare garden on a rare day,
and you are pinioned in the waterfall
from which the day would seem to rise.
I rise on the curl of your hair into ecstasy;
my love boat knocks from shore to dark green shore.
The birds go braying where I hide
      my intaglio of you.
This is my Mary lock and locket,
my chalice and the box I will not open.
Clearly, you have pruned me from your vines.
I know you through the earth's rising
and through the candles which you light
at your grandmother's grave.
Your red fruit defines a day you took from her bones,
sets my limits, calls my wedding bells.
Magdalene of the vine,
I would be free of the wicker of your day's duty,
your barter bays from dawn to twilight.
But in the waterfall's night, I hear you
call your familiar faces against me.
A Jesus of my continent veils your voices.
I am at rest as a shaker of serpents.
I once had a dervish depth to dapple you.
I once had my love's sorrow
      to draw you near me.
Now, I follow you down the sunshine,
and know the blood of the earth in the fruit,
the white pull of your bones upon the earth.
Now, here, I take the waterfall to wash
this stain of marriages from me.
I will not have you as my duty to the earth,
nor take the white pull of your bones
to reason with my days.
I have pitted your bare feet and wicker basket
against the jealous redness of my stripped love.
Unwed, I accept your turning of this our earth.

LOVE'S COLDNESS TURNS
TO THE WARMTH OF PATIENCE

My blanket smells of burnt apples.
My hair is tangled in smoky birch.
I sleep. I wake to watch the snow
ease itself around the shivering hills,
the same ice tick off in islands on the lake.
In all these silent postures,
I burrow into the memory of winter,
and fall, past your warmth,
into the high air of your heart.
Now, I am with you when the birds
circle and redeem their own air
and press the sun to hide their losses
in rainbows and serpent skins,
and, while you read their Zeno's flight,
I read your stillness.
                              I see now
in your eye the birds are bronzed
to be set near our temples in the wood.
Water and bronze, the birds curled on a staff
lead me to the purity of my own coldness,
down where what is lit is still unseen
and the blind light is the token
                              of your only star.
For who hopes for what he sees?
But if we hope for what we do not see,
we wait for it in patience.
I wait for the turning to teach me
what can be seen and what,
as I sit near my north star,
my lost green wood reveals.
I take the clothing of my memory's winter
as a sign that you are patient still.
Surely, I am my own flight into stillness
and into the cadence of a necessary cold.
I comfort you in the bed of charity,
my soul redeemed in your body's expected fire.

NEW ADAM'S CROSS

Dove, I offer you my hand,
and, from my shadows,
try to contain your sacred flight.
If I can name you or your flight,
I contain you. Berry lady,
I say love is your succulence.
Or are you my moonfall at the waterfall?
I know you are the blue bead
and the chicken kick, the diamond
or the gold stuck upon my stool.
At noon, I hear your frothy roll
bleat upon my grove's shores.
You come in the rain, you come in the wind,
you come in the eastern star; rose and redhead,
lily of the desert, my balm and blackness,
you surround me with your signs
and with your perfect body.
If now I am Adam,
you are my Eve of morning
and yet you cannot take your form
from my desire or from the gods' design.
I know my lure is useless.
I know I lie in shadows
because I cannot see your true light.
I say all light appears in darkness,
and every body rises against emptiness.
I say I know you through your mother
and my uncertain knowledge of her body
and her spirit. I know you as the web of my
father's spirit's weave and caress you
as the infinite water sign you weave.
Is love the name you weave?
And do I stand in the white milk of dawn
with only a red star for a sign
and watch my only horse split the air
and watch you wave your benediction at our backs?
And through your transparent body
can I see old palm leaves become

my first dwelling,
my first altar stone,
my first bride's first bed,
my fire,
my first grave?
Do I see you as the first example of my being,
or as the oldest road I take into my being?
You are the cross my body hangs
upon its spirit, the light my eyes will take
to read these oldest questions.
I am not all of you, you draw away from me.
I break my unillumined bones.

LOVE AS THE LIMIT AND GOAL

What in me is best
I lead to the hard stone
under the sun,
or to the dark habitation
of the blessed dead
where love's music
will be cut from my ear,
my body laid to serve
a constant light.
The subject of my own desire,
I am egg and synapse,
the body's pulsing measure,
the gold and purple of the light
about my days.
And so I invest myself,
invest you, with all
by which I dispossess you.
Now, when I beat my temple drum
and shake my bell
and praise my love in you,
I see the altar lock its heart
against your ecstasy.
The burden of the key,
under the rainbow,
rides you still.
You take the corn
for the thread of your skirt.
Love is the limit and the goal
by which that death is measured.
This love is the kinship of the saints
we bleed to make us worthy.
I turn from the order
of this constant dispossession
to awaken my body to the spirit's
historical sign, the logic of my soul
enlightened by your grounded eye.
I turn from possession of your oneness
to the vision of your twin acts,
the breaking of the ground from which I rise,
invested with the light my grave reveals.

INSCRUTABILITY

1

Inscrutable when I speak,
I am learning how my body sounds.
In the sand by the river's edge,
my head is a moon's egg,
my shell is a bell in my boat.
My arms and legs are storms.
I turn left, I turn right.
I chain myself with sun's rays,
star spur coals, bits of coal diamonds
and granite, a yucca branch,
a chicken claw and rose thorn;
I stretch goat hide between my arm and chest,
balata and steel from my lips,
and laud my women near the water.
The song I hear refers me to the mark
upon my body.
I hear my death again in nail rings.
I set the nail as harp of my breath.
Such music can be measured.
We have, then, a measure of zones
and generations, the association
of cloth and iron, herring bones and keys,
and, if I take my malt to the garden,
the glass contends with maguey,
the beads of crown and sceptre
recall an ascetic quarry.
But, temple bar, I inquire
how I am to examine you.
I have a measure for the facts,
but none for you.
Though I live in the essential
condition of vision,
what truth I know
is a burden in my ear,
sign and countersign
of the light's discoveries.
Light is a weight in the ear,
a memory of the light's incisions,

and, in the dark, I clear
my possession of memory's poles
with the attributes of speech.
Then, if the god speaks of failure,
I tune my body's speech star-high.
I work the dead from darkness
into light; for these
there is no other definition.
Darkness and silence define
a lover on a bed,
or shuttled in a tree,
a constellation of beads,
bridal veils and berries.
I hear in the contradiction
of my song, a weeping.
My speech is a plumb line
to the echo of the earth.
My voice survives on a dervish dance,
and a king's howling body
would be the first stone of my house.
These are the deeds
to possession of my body;
these are the acts
by which I dispossess myself.
I remain a morph in my own
                              proposition.
Clearly,
my leaving and return
are in my power.
I number my powers
by an inscrutable class—
my voice in the leaves of a river
in which my light and full
and silent body lies.
I ask how to measure
the leaving and return,
the weight of the body.
I ask which of the marks I must
perceive to enhance my speaking.
I examine, now, the exactness
of salvation, proverb and purpose,
the blaze of the serpent skin.
I am persuaded of spring oats

and corn and barley, wine
and sweetmeats, darkness
and this text on light and the dark.
I speak only what is sufficient
and what can be assured
by the essential condition of vision.
I am in the place of light,
a bell in my own boat,
storm-driven into speech,
and, by the rhythm of desire,
I forge my body's space.
I refer to the unity of this space,
and to my body's singular paradigm.
But even here, I wait with you
for the bird's flight into meaning.

2

(i)

This must be said.
I am provoked by the state of things.
On the most propitious night,
the mother claims her god's
singular visit; the results
are the birds you see before you.
Bird, I know you as a common thief
of fish, a puller of nets in the dawn.
You cannot fly by your hungers.
But the god assures your holiness.
Our speech assures your struggle
with the god; your body addresses
this schema of our own desires.
You are the rain's head, the solitary
prayer in the brass-filled temple,
the mutilated tree on the rainless hills.
If you are silent,
we turn that silence to a tilling tool,
an eave, a hearth, or a pot.
We wear your silence against the heat.
We tune our day's bells to your pauses.

Your every proposition is grace,
a perfection of our absences.
Twin, you title all my voiceless provocations.
And yet I am indifferent to the terms
you choose, until I choose them.
Changer, fox, a fallen verb,
even you provoke my speech.
I ignore your generation.
Determined,
I begin again to parse my body's needs.
I ask if the world is real enough
to measure my intention.

(ii)

Down where the smallest quality
will turn and figure itself,
turn again to become other than itself,
I hear the exact belling of my vexation.
(Strange, how I refer to every act as sound.)
I body all my logic of the world
in the gray depths of these changes.
I pull the world's bare figures
to the scaffold of my gray eye.
I am, in the form of my own urging,
my gray eye and, in its movement,
I have my schemes, my launch-pad
                              into the actual.
If the god's elemental bones are real,
my hand must never scruple to design his flesh.
Old men will have it
that the word alone is real,
and leave these facts in pieces.
Is the word the design of the fragments,
or of the strict connection of the missing fact?
Surely, a yeoman would search another tree,
or the leaf fallen from the same tree.
Thing is not a name, and a tree
is named by virtue of its life.
You must consider that the tree has changed.
The tree alone can never bear semblance
to such a stripped body.

I assert now the eye is a pauper;
crown it, and subtract the self.
The English, impersonal banker retreats,
is content, is at home, is heard no more.
If I am intelligible as the other,
I explore my body's future path.
I become the body's changing form,
transformed by any unspoken absence.
The act itself is figure and ground
for the necessary absence.
Then we must go down,
through the will of the dead,
and ride the living mind to the dance
of light, distinguish the tune
in which our names are called.

(iii)

Still, I am entranced
by the eye's harmonics—
soundings of the invisible;
historical return;
field of the line and counterline;
false note and true;
house of fact and composition;
sphere in the wall of two lights.
Old opposites possess me once again.
I surrender and contest
my power to enhance you,
my need to embrace you as you are.
Are you the ring in the peacock's tail,
the round stone temple on an arid
mountain, the black belly of a fish
in moon rings? Are you a footprint
glazed on the urn of the sand,
the litter-shield of a warrior's body,
a bride in a white hut,
the drum or its message of love?
Voiceless rainbows speak in their colors.
The wind rides its horse
up the cobbled streets at noon.
Up, down. All figures rise or fall.

They arrive before me.
They remain.
I remain, a sinew in an aggressive hip,
the counterweight to another speaker's
                              exultant eye.
You must adjust to this intensity.
In the tumult of this body's vision,
I must elicit my intention.

(iv)

I am arguing with the body's exaltation
and the mind's enstoolment on the seat of love,
all inebriate devices of the fallen.
I cling to the fate of taking one step
at a time, or so I say, and know I lie.
I lie by the process of enacting my memories.
You are in these acts.
I cite your losses; I cite your powers.
We devise the truth of all
                    we have not learned.
It has been given to us to understand
what may only be spoken.
What is unspoken may be undone,
what is undone may be unspoken.
I am proposing the clarity
of the undone, the still unspoken,
the clarity of stillness in the movement,
of the movement in the perfect calm.
I am proposing the undetermined body,
the invested space.
I cite the ages of liberation—
from the key,
from the second eye,
from sainthood
and from death,
from the body's definition
and its investment,
from the quality of being actual.
I bring you every disposition
of the double.
You will not find my sign

bare in your gray eye,
nor shivering feebly and alone
in your ear,
but bodied in the deep ground
of my tongue's impossible passage
through the ill-defined logic
of my body's exaltation.

NOTE

The ideograms in the poem, "MacIntyre, the Captain and the Saints," were suggested by Mr. Robert L. Wilson's use of ideograms in a short series of his unpublished poems. Mr. Wilson uses the basic ideogram □ . . . ⊟ to indicate the opening and closing of the frame. For him, in ideogrammatic notation, there are three kinds of a basic identity: 1) external, in which the ideogram undergoes a shift in meaning effected by the context; 2) internal, in which the context undergoes a shift in meaning in relation to the ideogram; 3) mixed, a reciprocal shift in meaning. Internal ideograms are primary; external are secondary. What has attracted me to the ideograms is their ability to mark clearly the transformation of meaning in a dramatic poem such as mine. The ideograms need not be used in every poem, but it seems to me that they are particularly useful in this one. I have, therefore, adapted Mr. Wilson's ideograms to my own peculiar ones in order to make even more radical distinctions among the temporal and spatial voices in the poem. I have used > . . . < for internal, * . . . ‡ and ** . . . ** for external and / . . . / for mixed ideograms. Mr. Wilson has tried to save me from these errors by suggesting a basic ideogram which could be distinguished by simple secondary markers, but I have trudged ahead with my own ideogrammatic weight. It seems to me appropriate that, for the clarification of my personal Scottish intellectual drama, I should have at hand an inventive technique elaborated by a citizen of brave Dundee and that he should have found his initiative in reading Ezra Pound, the universalist of ideograms. I am grateful to Mr. Wilson for his license to use his ideas, and for his understanding manner toward the license I have taken to use them.

The reader will recognize the poem's four actors as Wright; Capt. R.S. Rattray, a British Colonial Administrator and Scot, who headed the first Anthropological Department established by that government in what he called Ashanti, West Africa; Hugh MacDiarmid, or Christopher Murray Grieve, a great Scottish poet, shaper of the Lallans Scots language and national sensibility; David Hume, British philosopher and historian.

Among the many texts which I have had in hand, some were essential and may be of interest and help to the reader. I give a short list, with the reminder that though these have helped

to shape my poem, they are not, individually or collectively,
my poem.

R.S. Rattray, *Ashanti*

R.S. Rattray, *Religion and Art in Ashanti*

Hugh MacDiarmid, *A Drunk Man Looks at the Thistle*

David Hume, *An Inquiry Concerning Human Understanding*

David Hume, *A Treatise of Human Nature, Book One, Of the
Understanding.*

Rosalind Mitchison, *A History of Scotland*

T.C. Smout, *A History of the Scottish People, 1560-1830*

A final great presence stands behind my poem: J.B. Dan-
quah, Ghanaian politician, philosopher/theologian, sociologist
and historian. His *Akan Doctrine of God*, for all its faults, is
a true book of wisdom, one of deeply human and transcen-
dent aesthetic and spiritual knowledge. My poem is an attempt,
among other things, to claim this knowledge as part of the con-
tinuing creative life of the Americas.